Saint or Sinner?

How God Deals with the Sins of His Saints

Saint or Sinner?

How God Deals with the Sins of His Saints

by

Clifton Coulter

Introduction
Updated and Revised in 2016

by Geri Coulter

When my husband first received this revelation of God's unconditional love and His marvelous grace, and the fact that our sins are forgiven once and for all, he was one of a very few preaching this outrageous message. I am happy to say that this truth has spread now, and many are preaching the grace of God. This is the truth: we have unmerited favor that has been ours from the beginning.

For me, one of the most powerful points in this message is the teaching on I John 1:9. This impactful point has been revealed to many men and women of God sovereignly, without them even seeking such a thing.

The contents of this book are based on a message Clifton taught in Kansas City in 1995. Many thanks to Dennis and Denise Capra for pushing this project through to completion. Thanks to Grace Perry Szilvasy for the original transcription and to Steve

Corgan for his help to format and put it into book form.   Brian Jenkins was the original publisher. Thanks also to Rick and Judi Manis for publishing this revised edition.

Table of Contents

Chapter One
A Better Covenant

The book of Hebrews simply points to a better covenant. It begins talking about that from the first chapter. Then, in the ninth chapter, it begins to deal with sin and with what we typically refer to as sin.

Then verily the first covenant had also ordinances of divine service, and a worldly sanctuary. For there was a tabernacle made, the first, wherein was the candlestick, and the table, and the shewbread; which is called the sanctuary. After that, the second veil, the tabernacle which is called the Holiest of all; Which had the golden sensor, and the ark of the covenant overlaid round about with gold, wherein was the golden pot that had manna, and Aaron's rod that budded, and the tables of the covenant. And over it, the cherubims of glory shadowing the mercy seat, of which we cannot now speak particularly. (Hebrews

9:1-5)

But into the second went the high priest alone once every year, not without blood which he offered for himself, and for the errors of the people. (Hebrews 9:7)

I don't know if you have ever heard anybody say anything like this before, but I have not confessed a sin since 1990. Before you get shocked over that, I'm not saying I have not sinned since then. Don't ask me if I've sinned. I'm saying it has been all these years since I confessed a sin. There's a reason for that, and when you begin to see it, it will be a completely different teaching than you have been used to hearing. A few years ago, I began to see it. I saw I John 1:9 in a completely different light. I realized that John was not talking to someone who was born again when he said to confess sin. He was talking to someone who believed in God, but had not yet accepted Jesus Christ.

I travel all over the world. One of the things I see that is hindering Christians more than anything is that they are walking around with an old sin consciousness and a guilt-ridden attitude. They are in fear they have done something to displease God. And because of that, they feel they can't be used of God. And, yes, it is true that we do things wrong. There's no question about that. And we should have godly sorrow that would bring us to repentance. We should tell God we are sorry. But I believe for us, as Christians, if we go around all the time confessing sin and calling ourselves sinners, we can never rid ourselves of a sin consciousness. And that is exactly what the writer is talking about here in the book of Hebrews. It talks about how God views someone on this side of the cross. I like to say it this way: There was a time we were on the other side of the cross. But when we passed through the cross to the other side of it, we became like the resurrected Jesus! We died on that cross, too. Our old man was crucified on that cross. On this side of the cross, sin has been dealt with. On the other side of the cross, sin still had not been dealt with.

This was the reason for the cross. It is just that simple. There had to be a cross. There had to be a second tree to take care of what happened concerning the first tree. The first Adam picked up that sin, and the second Adam came as Jesus Christ, and took care of the sin. The handwriting and ordinances of the law

3

and everything else that was against us was nailed to that tree.

The law came in after God had made a covenant with Abraham. The promise to Abraham was that God was going to restore the spirit back to man, not as unto "seeds" but to his "Seed," which was Jesus. So God made a covenant with Abraham. He found someone with faith, someone who would hold onto the promise. God told him to hold onto it, and keep the covenant before the people, and through his seed He was going to bring the promise. The promise was that God was going to place His Spirit back inside of man, the one that Adam lost on the first tree (The Tree of Knowledge of Good and Evil).

Chapter Two
The Perfect Sacrifice

The reason Jesus was the perfect sacrifice to die on the cross for us, and to be that perfect sacrifice, was not necessarily because He did everything perfect, although we are not contesting that. But the reason He was the perfect sacrifice was because He was the only Person on earth who was born of the seed of God. Everyone else was born of the seed of Adam. And do you know what God called that? God said that was merciful. He said He was going to have mercy on everyone. Therefore, He made everyone a sinner.

On that side of the cross, everyone was a sinner. There are still people on that side of the cross that are still sinners. But on this side of the cross, no one is a sinner. To clear that up, read Hebrews 6-10. It says that Jesus died for the sins of the Old Testament, the old covenant. Therefore if He died for the sins of the Old Testament, and we say He died for our sins: past, present, and future, then what does that do with the future sins? What does that do with the present tense sins? As far as God is concerned, we are not sinners. He dealt with that sin, because it was never really our sin that made us a sinner in the first place. If we could ever get it into our heads that "sinning" is not what made us sinners, then we would understand that "doing right" is not what makes us righteous. Romans 6:20 explains that when we were sinners we were free from righteousness. I don't want to be free from righteousness!

We think of freedom as being set free from a trap. But here, free just means I couldn't get to it. I was free from it. I couldn't get there. There was no way I could get to righteousness when I was a sinner. It was not because I was "doing sin." I was a sinner because I was born of the seed of Adam. Since I was born of the seed of Adam, I was a sinner, not because I sinned, but because I was born in sin. I didn't have to sin to become a sinner. God made it merciful on me. If God had not made it that way, somebody would say, "I never sinned." But because God made it that way, when somebody does say that, He can say, "The truth isn't in you." *If we say that we have no sin, we deceive ourselves, and the truth is not in us.* (I John 1:18) He made us all sinners so He could have mercy on all of us the same way. If He made us all sinners the same way, then He could have mercy and make us all righteous the same way.

People say, "I don't see how I can be righteous when I haven't done anything right." Well, how was Jesus made a sinner when He didn't do anything wrong? It's God. God did that. It's one of those things we can't understand. God did it. And so when you think about how Jesus died for the sins of the Old Testament, then that tells me that as far as God is concerned, on this side of the cross there aren't any sins for Jesus to die for. There is no sin on this side of the cross as far as God is concerned.

When I was a sinner, I was free from righteousness. I couldn't get to righteousness. Could I do anything good? Yes, I could do good things. And was that good I did beneficial to myself and others? Only to the world I was living in. It only had an effect in this horizontal environment, but there is also a vertical relationship that we have with God which was made through Jesus. There is a horizontal relationship we have with one another. The vertical relationship was made through Jesus alone. Works and deeds have nothing to do with that. There was not one thing we could ever do to get that relationship. That's why man was hopeless and helpless without God. We didn't have any hope or faith in our hearts. We didn't have any hope at all without Jesus. Then Jesus came along and made all this possible. He called it mercy. It doesn't make any difference whether you are big, little, smart, dumb, tall, short, skinny or fat. God was going to put everyone in the same boat, so that the only way to get out of that boat was to get into the new one He had prepared. And when we get into this one, everyone will be in the same boat again. It's a boat of righteousness. He accomplished this brilliant rescue through Jesus. He did not do it through works or based on our performance.

When I was a sinner, I couldn't get to righteousness. There was not anything I could do to get to righteousness. I could do right, and I could do a lot of good things. Geri and I are good people, but did you know I was a drunk? I didn't beat my wife, though. And I was good to my kids. But I was a drunk. I couldn't reach the cross. There wasn't any way. I could do good, and that helped my neighbor. That good helped my wife. Proverbs is a book that talks about how to get along in this world, but you could do everything in Proverbs and it would never save you. But would your neighbor like you? Yeah, he would. Your wife would like you, your husband would like you, and even your dog would like you, because you would not pick him up by his ears! Doing the things Proverbs teaches is a good way to learn to get along in life. But it won't save you. Proverbs teaches the wisdom of the world.

Solomon asked God for wisdom to be able to judge the people, and to understand things. And that's what God gave him. Solomon was called the wisest man in the world. He wrote the Proverbs. He had the wisdom of the world. He knew how to get along in the world. Did that cut any ice with God? No, not really. Yes, He loved him anyway, that is easy to say. God loves everybody. But do you see what I am saying? Are you getting the big picture?

Chapter 3

Which Side of the Cross Are You On?

I was free from righteousness. If I did everything in the book of Proverbs, I would be a very good person. You could tell someone who wasn't even saved, "Study the book of Proverbs, apply it to your life, and you will be a good person." He/she would have a lot of worldly wisdom, and could probably stay out of trouble, but it still would do no good as far as reaching God. He would still be free from righteousness, because he would still be on that side of the cross.

You see, I was able to do good. But my doing good was not able to make me righteous. It benefited me on this earth. Now I am on this side of the cross. I went from being free from righteousness to this side of the cross. Now I'm free from sin. Can I make myself a sinner? I can't make myself a sinner by what I do any more than I can make myself righteous by what I did on the other side of the cross. If Christians could ever get a hold of this, they would quit doing some of the things they are doing. This is what will set you free from sin. It won't cause you to want to go out and sin more. It will cause you to say, "Wait a minute, I have been giving in to the flesh, I have been giving in to pressure, I have been giving in to the law." The law gives strength to sin. I Corinthians 15:56 says: *The sting of death is sin, and the power of sin is the law.* I realized that I'd been doing stuff that I didn't have to do. God doesn't even see me doing those things. Boy, is that good news or what?

People sometimes say, "Brother, what you preach gives folks a license to sin." Actually, that would be the best thing we could do for Christians. At least it would give them some relief for awhile. Because they're sinning anyway, and if they found out it didn't make a difference regarding their acceptance with God, they would quit doing those things.

The Bible says it is the law that gives strength to sin. If there is pressure on you to not sin all the time, it is because you are legalistic, and you are afraid that God is going to hate you, and be angry if you sin. Perhaps you think that when you do something good, this is the only time He loves you or is pleased with you. And that's why you have this complex. You don't understand how much God truly loves you. That's why you feel this way. The solution to that dilemma is this righteousness message you are reading about now.

If you are like me, you may have read I John 3 and gotten to the part that says: *Whosoever abideth in Him sinneth not,* and then just closed the book. I thought I abided in Him until I read that. It goes on to say such things as: *whosoever sinneth has not seen Him, neither has known Him.* Do you know Him? Have you already been saved? Well, then you are not a sinner. See, we missed the whole point. It says that he that abides in Him sins not. You're free from sin. It would be the same thing if we turned it around and said, "He who does good is free from righteousness."

This chapter in I John starts out by trying to show us that God loves us so much that He allowed us to call ourselves sons of God. I John 3: 1-2 says: *Behold what manner of love the Father has bestowed on us, that we should be called the sons of God...it does not yet appear what I shall be, but when He appears, I shall be like Him.* Has He appeared to you? Yes, He has already appeared to you. This is something that has already taken place. Jesus has already appeared to you. He has already appeared to me. And so I am just like Him, I'm without sin.

In Hebrews we see that every time in the Old Covenant that there was a confession, there was a sacrifice. If Jesus had been the same high priest as these guys were when they had to offer a sacrifice every year, it says He would have suffered from the foundation of the earth. But He died once at the end of this world. Jesus died once for all. There's no more sacrifice. If you make a confession, you have to make a sacrifice. We're not going to sacrifice Jesus again.

The Israelite people really believed God loved them. The problem was they had become so religious and strict that the love was not flowing through them to other people. They had lost sight of God, and Jesus had to come and show them what God was like again. They were still the best people on earth. They weren't evil people. They were good people, and their goodness benefited them, just like it would benefit us on that side of the cross. They were blessed and they had everything. They were wealthy. They had kept the commandments. They did a lot of things that God had told them to do. But that goodness, that strict good behavior, was smothering all the people who could not do those things. It smothered them out, and they saw God as cruel and mean and regimented. And so Jesus had to come and show them what God was really like.

Chapter Four
You Are God's Seed

Jesus came to earth, but when He started going to the downtrodden and the ones who were hurting, the Pharisees said, "This can't be Him." The very people who said they knew God could not recognize Him. The way Jesus was behaving just did not fit their chart for God. Man's opinion of God had gotten far away from the way He really was. But God still loved them then, and God still loves them today.

Once a year they had to go back and offer a sacrifice, and once a year they were reminded that they were sinners. However, because they were reminded one time a year that they were sinners, the sacrifice still could not rid them of an evil conscience. If a person could not be rid of an evil conscience when he was reminded only once a year that he was a sinner, what does that say to us who think we have to confess our sins all the time?

First John 1:9 (*If we confess our sins, he is faithful and just to forgive us our sins, and to cleanse us from all unrighteousness*) is the only place in the New Testament where it implies that someone who has been converted should again confess sin. Why is this important? If God thought it was important enough to say that we are going to have to have a purer blood than goats and calves and bulls to get people rid of an evil conscience, then I think this is serious. Saying something like that will get me thrown out of most churches, that is if I came preaching this. You ask, "What has this done for you, not confessing your sins for years?" It has set me free. I don't worry about whether I am doing something wrong or right. Yes, we are to do things right, there is no question about that. We should try to be the best that we can be. But when I do something wrong, it does not make me a sinner any more than when I did things right, it did not make me righteous. You need to get to the place where you see yourself free from sin. The Bible says that sin is transgressing the law (see I John 4:4).

At one time the state of Montana did not have a speed limit. If I was in Montana when there was no speed limit, I could drive as fast as I wanted to. Would I be speeding? No, because there was no law telling me I was speeding. I couldn't speed in Montana. That's what it means when I John 3:6 states: *He who abides in Him sins not.* You don't sin because you can't sin. Keep in mind this is from God's point of view. I know this is hard on our brains, but the Bible says if you are born of His Seed, you can't sin. We talk contrary to that all the time, but that is what the Bible says. Take it up with Him. I didn't write it. I had interpreted I John 1:9 the way it had been taught to me for years and I was miserable. What's the difference now? I am happy now. I am free. I don't ever go to God wondering whether He loves me. God is not holding anything against us. If He were, we are all in big trouble, because when you get God against you, who can be for you? He is not against us. He took all the "againstness" out on the cross. He put it all on Jesus. Everything that was against us, He put on Jesus, and Jesus paid the price for all of us, once and for all. If we think we need to confess sins every day, what does that say about the blood of Jesus? When we think that we need to add some work of our own to perfect our salvation, or to make it better, it is the same thing as taking this precious blood of Jesus and mixing it with a little goat blood to improve it. We wouldn't do that. Nevertheless, that is what the Bible says we are doing when we act and think like I've described here. We are saying that the blood of Jesus wasn't as good as goat blood. It wasn't as good as cow blood. I know we don't think that. Nobody thinks that, but most of the time we act like that's what we believe.

When I first started seeing this, I'd go to bed and I would say, "Hallelujah, Lord, I just thank you that I'm forgiven. I thank you Father, that you are holding nothing against me. I thank you that I am loved like you say in your Word, and that I can do anything. I can do all things through Christ who strengthens me. I don't have to worry whether I am worthy to talk to you."

Look how easy He made it. He said we have not a high priest who cannot be touched with the feelings of our infirmities, but was in all points tempted as we were, but without sin. He was without sin. When Satan tempted Jesus, the first thing he tempted Him with was basically to say, "If you are really the Son of God, do something to prove it." Do something. Jesus had just come from a baptism. His own. God had spoken out of Heaven and said: *This is My Beloved*

Son, in whom I am well pleased (see Matthew 3:17).
The only thing Jesus had done up to this point was to
be born. That's the only thing He had done. He had
not performed one miracle when God spoke out of
Heaven saying He was pleased with His Son. Do you
know why God was pleased with Jesus? It's because
Jesus was God's seed. You are God's seed now, and
He is saying he same thing to you. He is saying the
same thing to you because you are His seed, not
because of anything you have done or haven't done.
He loves you because you are His seed.

Chapter Five
Hid in Christ

You were born of God and you can't sin because there is no law against the Spirit that is in you. There is no law against it. What do you think Galatians 5:23 is referring to when it says: *Against such there is no law?* It's the fruit of the Spirit. There is no law against the freedom that God has given you. Law causes bondage. Law causes death. There is a spirit of bondage that has been put on all of us. I was talking to someone today who told me she came out of a very rigid church. These churches have people in them who love God with all their hearts, with everything that is in them, but they are scared. They are afraid and they are in bondage. We've all been that way, afraid of God. However, He said we have a High Priest and He is so merciful. He says we can come to His throne boldly. It's called the throne of grace. The Bible says we can go there and find mercy and grace to help in time of need.

Just think about this. There is an altar you can run to any time and receive from it. There is nothing there that is going to harm you. You can run to the throne of God and come away smelling like a rose. You are going to get what you don't deserve, and you are never going to get what you do deserve. You go to the throne of grace and get unmerited favor, and you don't get justice. I don't want to get what I deserve! Aren't you glad we are not getting what we deserve? When we run to the throne of God, we are in need of some help. Do you run to God and say, "Oh, God, I'm just here?" No. When you feel like that you go to the shopping mall.

Why would we be afraid of God when He is trying to tell us we have a High Priest who knows how we feel? He knows what it's like to be tempted to do something to prove that we're right with God. He said, "I was tempted on all those points, but I did not become a sinner. You can believe you are everything I say you are because it's not based on your performance." That's good news!

You are clothed in His righteousness. To illustrate

this point, I'll relate a personal story. I was in a motel room and I was talking to God. I had been invited to minister in a place that was high on my esteem list and I said, "God, if this person knew me like I know me, he would never have asked me to come." And God said, "I know it." I fell out of bed and began to confess my sins and everybody else's (this was before I quit confessing sin).

After awhile I stopped, and God said, "I don't even know you like you know yourself." He doesn't see us with our un-renewed minds. He sees us with His renewed mind. He sees us through Jesus. The only time you are in agreement with God is when you are talking like He does. If God says you're not a sinner, and you say you are a sinner, then you are not in agreement with God. If you are seeing yourself as a sinner, then you haven't renewed your mind. You've still got a sin consciousness. You've still got an evil conscience. You still think it's the things you do right that make you right with God and that it's the things you do wrong that make you wrong with God. You've still got that old un-renewed mind.

God said to me, "I don't see you that way. You're hid in Christ." I said, "Hid?" He said, "Yes, you're hid in

Christ in Me." So I asked Him, "Who am I hid from?"
I knew it was not the devil because he found me. I
was not hidden from my own thoughts because they
were there. No, you are not hidden from the devil and
you're not hidden from your own thoughts. Do you
know who you are hidden from? Him! You say, "I
don't want to be hidden from God." You must realize
this: you are hidden from Him, but you are also
hidden in Him. He took the part of me He couldn't
look at anymore and He hid it in Himself. And when
He looks at me, He does not see that. He sees Jesus.
So then, being the intelligent man that I am, I had to
get into the Word to see if it was true. When God tells
me something, I've got to prove it in the Word, and I
found it taught in Paul's letter to the Colossians.

In this case, I wasn't sure where the error in my
thinking came from. Did it come from the devil or
my own thoughts? I'd always been proud that I could
tell the difference. If the devil, as he has been
depicted, would come walking through that door with
his horns out and flames flying, a pitchfork tail and
evil eyes and all of that, and walked up to you, telling
you how wrong you are and how bad you are, you
would say, "Well, you're the devil, I'm not going to
believe you." You wouldn't believe what he said,

would you? I once had a woman say to me that the devil was telling her this and that, and she kept talking about it. I just stood there and looked at her. It was a preacher's wife. She was in a panic, and just kept on and on. Finally I said, "Did you hear what you just said?" She said, "What?" I said, "You said the devil was saying this stuff." She said, "Yes." I said, "Well, you should be glad. That is good news! He's a liar! You should be tickled that he is saying all of that, because you can turn it all around and believe just the opposite."

But in this particular instance, I wanted to know if it was the devil talking to me, because if it was, I would arm myself against that. But if it was me, what do I do about my own thinking? After all, I am the one who knows me. That's not what the Bible says, but that's what I was thinking. The Bible says that the Spirit knows you. Who knows a man except the spirit of a man? That's not referring to the "soulish" realm of a man, but the spirit realm of a man. My spirit bears witness. I've got the Spirit in there telling my spirit that I am the son of God. Finally my spirit is getting a hold of this. And my mind is beginning to get a hold of it. I said, "God, I want to know, was that the devil or was that me?" He said, "It doesn't make any difference, you're both wrong." What a revelation! You mean I'm wrong if I am agreeing with the devil? Then that must mean I'm right if I am agreeing with God. That's renewing your mind.

Chapter Six
You're Not Guilty

Anytime my mind is in agreement with anything the devil is telling me, I am wrong. It doesn't make any difference whether the devil says it or not. You might say, "Wait a minute, the devil wasn't there, I did it on my own." It doesn't make any difference. If you are guilty, then you don't have the revelation of righteousness. You've not renewed your mind to righteousness.

We're not guilty. As far as God is concerned, you are not guilty. Is it possible for me to do wrong on this side of the cross? Yes. Does it make me wrong with God? No. Does my wrongdoing make me a sinner? No. Can it cause me trouble? Yes, it can cause me a lot of trouble. Why would you want to confess all the things you are in God and then not act like it? Ephesians 1 says we are holy, blameless, righteous, blessed, and have an inheritance. We are healed, prosperous, and have the joy of the Lord. We are to confess these things. We've been trying to act like it so we can believe it. We need to believe it then act like it. Believing will change what you do, but doing will not change what you believe. You can do stuff forever, and it won't change what you believe.

I am not a sinner. Therefore I don't have any reason to go to God and give myself an old complex of sin consciousness by confessing the things I do wrong. Many times when I start teaching this out of I John, people think I am saying that poor old John didn't know what he was talking about. I think John knew exactly what he was talking about. I think it is *us* who haven't realized who he was talking *to*.

If you look again and really study this chapter, you will realize that he is speaking to someone who has not yet received the fullness of Jesus. I believe he was talking to someone who believed in God, such as a Jewish brother who had not accepted Jesus.

John said: *I want to share these things with you, because truly my fellowship is with the Father and with his Son Jesus Christ* (see I John 1:3). This guy could relate to the "Father" if he was Jewish, but John wanted him to see there was more for him to grasp. True fellowship with the Father includes fellowship with His Son, Jesus Christ.

John further explains: *God is light, and in Him is no darkness at all.* When we were walking on that side of the cross, as this guy was, we were in darkness. A true believer has been translated from darkness into this marvelous light. He said if you say you're in the light, but you are walking in darkness, then that's not right. You can't do that. What he is saying is that there's not two different ways to walk.

It's not talking about what you do; it's talking about what you believe. Do you believe in Jesus? Do you trust Him for your salvation, or are you just walking in darkness believing that the law is going to save you? That is what he is talking about. And then he goes on to say: *If we are walking in the light as he is in the light...* In other words, if we receive the truth of what he has done for us, if we'll walk in the light as He is in the light, we have fellowship with one another and the blood of Jesus cleanses us from all sin. So, when I am walking with Jesus, I am cleansed. Am I walking in the truth? Yes, I believe in Jesus.

Didn't He say: *I am the Way, the Truth, and the Life?* (John 14:6) My salvation is in Jesus, and His blood keeps me clean. I don't have to go and confess.

He was talking to somebody else when he said: *If you say you haven't sinned, the truth is not in you. But if you confess your sins, God is faithful and just to forgive your sins and cleanse you from all unrighteousness* (see I John 1:8-9). Think about this: when would a person need to be cleansed from all unrighteousness? Before he/she was saved! John went on to say: *If we say we have not sinned, we make Him a liar, and His word is not in us* (I John 1:10). You do not believe the Word if you say you are not a sinner, if you are saying you don't need Jesus. Then, in the next chapter, it says: *My little children I write these things to you that you sin not.* Again, we think that means, "I shouldn't sin." No, what he is saying is, "I write these things to you that you are not a sinner." But if you do sin, if you do something wrong, you have an advocate with the Father. Now, we've either got an advocate with the Father, or we have to run and confess sins all the time. Which is it?

I'm not saying this to be humble, but I am really not that intelligent as far as book knowledge is concerned.

But I am a practical person. I do believe I have a lot of common sense. I don't have to analyze everything. I believe that God makes sense. I believe He loves me. I don't believe He has anything against me. And it's not because of me. It's because of Jesus. I'm just simple enough to believe that. It has changed my life, and it has made me happy. I've been ministering for years, and I feel I just now have the truth.

You might be saved and be miserable. There's a freedom in Jesus that I can't express. I can't get it out, but it is all through the Word. What we have done over the years is, we have "versed" the Bible. We have taken a verse here, and a verse there, and made it read the way we wanted it to read, or the way somebody has taught us to read it. We need to get back into the book and read the whole thing. We should read Paul's letters as letters. Don't just pull a scripture out and say this is what he meant. Read all of it. There is a theme that runs through it: grace and peace. Go back and get the "big picture." Did God really want to redeem man? Did God really want a man He could have fellowship with? Did God want someone He could lavish His love on? *Behold what manner of love the Father has bestowed upon us, that we would be called the sons of God.* (I John 3:1)

Satan loves to get a hold of an old bound-up Christian, sitting around feeling sorry for himself, feeling guilty, wondering why he's so unworthy...while the rest of the world is dying and going to hell. The sorriest Christian in here is better off than the best lost man out there. I have had people whine and cry to me saying, "Well, Brother Coulter, I don't feel like my light is too bright." My response is to say, "Well, Praise God, go to a darker place. I could take you places where you would shine like a beacon."

We need to get our focus off of ourselves. This teaching will get you off of yourself. Quit trying to cover your tracks and start making some. Quit trying to back up and cover up what is behind you. God loves you. God cares about you. If He didn't, we'd all be in trouble. He's got a plan for your life. And it's not that you keep trying to get good enough for Him. It's taking His goodness to other people.

Epilogue
Clifton and Geri Living It

by Geri Coulter

After all these years of living "sin-conscious-free," we can honestly say that this life of freedom has opened up a whole new world to us. As for me, Geri, I do not ever think about sin. It does not plague me even though, of course, I know I do not do everything perfectly. My mind is free to think about God, His Spirit, and what He would have me to do to fulfill my destiny. Clifton feels the same way. We know we have an assignment from God to propagate the gospel, to make the kingdom bright on the earth through our witness and life. This cannot happen with a sin consciousness; nor can it happen with a fear or dread of punishment. To say you are sorry and move on is sufficient for God as far as the believer is concerned. To weep and wail at the altar of His presence over your wrongdoing is to say that the blood of Jesus was not enough. If you allow sin to dominate your thinking, you have not received the truth of the power that is in the precious blood of Jesus. "How can I do this or how can I make the switch?" you may ask. For me, I think it was through concentrating on worshiping Him and being thankful for all He has done for me.

God is the most amazing One I know. His promises are true! As we shed off the consciousness of the old nature and begin to walk in who we truly are, we will see miracles and we will see the normal Christian life unfold. We might think, "Oh, this is a miracle!" when in truth, it is just the normal life of one who is a believer. It is normal for us to see those around us healed through our prayers. It is the normal Christian life to see miracles and to see favor and blessing on ourselves and all those around us!

Let me give an example. Clifton and I have always preached prosperity. We have believed that God wanted us prosperous, and all our needs met. We have believed that there should be abundance for us, and enough to give and help others. For many years we struggled with not having enough finances to do everything we wanted to do. I speak here of the things God was leading us to do. We always went forward, even if we did not have what we felt we needed. We took released prisoners into our home and fed them and trained them, and used what we had to minister to them. Our goal and heart was to have a place for the abuser of drugs and alcohol. We even had a name: "House of Hope." We brought them to our own home.

Our vision for "Operation Word" was to minister to the terminally ill. It was fulfilled by our own church people going into homes where those suffering were prayed for and the Word read to them. We also performed regular household chores. In one case, we canned a whole garden for a family because the patient was so sick.

My point is we just kept going. Finally, after all these years we know how to believe, and how to continue to walk in the knowledge that God takes care of His kids, and He takes care of us. If we need money, God gets it to us. We live in a nice home, we drive nice vehicles, our freezer and refrigerator are full and we have everything we need. Our ministry is blessed.

Learning to walk in His provision and blessing is a great reward. We never waste time praying for money. We don't receive money by praying. No one does. We receive money by giving and expecting.

Living sin-free opens your mind and heart to receive from God the way He wants you to, without fear of what He thinks of you. He thinks you are awesome! He loves you so much He gave His son for you. He has a lot invested in you, and He is not going to treat you badly!

You are complete in Him. He has given you everything. Since He gave His Son for you, how much more will He freely give you all things? (See Romans 8:32)

Our final encouragement to you is to think upon the things written here. Grace and righteousness are available to everyone! We appropriate everything God has provided by our faith. By believing. By trusting that God has told us the truth.

About the Author

Clifton Coulter has a background of "sinner." That's what he told the denominational board of directors when they were interviewing him to see if he could qualify to be a minister in their organization. "What is your background?" they asked.

His background was that he had been an alcoholic and "bar room brawler." The description was one given to him by the "700 Club" when they came to our home to interview us in the 80's. His testimony was aired around the world for years.

Clifton and Geri were born again in 1970, answered the call to ministry in April of 1977 and began to preach immediately. Along with three other families, they pioneered a church, *The Lighthouse*, in Paoli Indiana in August of 1977.

Since then, the Coulters have been around the world in thirteen nations preaching and conducting Marriage Conferences and Evangelistic Services. They have spread the gospel on radio, TV, and have taken the Word in person across the United States. Geri continues with a radio broadcast, "Oasis of Love," in their hometown of Paoli Indiana. She is a popular Ladies Conference speaker. They have been instructors at a Bible College in Colorado and in their own School of Ministry in Missouri.

Presently Clifton pastors *Grace Family Outreach Church* in Park Hills Missouri. He continues to travel and teach the unconditional love of God. Soul winning is still his passion.

The Coulters live in Farmington, Missouri. They have four children, twelve grandchildren, and two great grandchildren. Clifton and Geri have been married for 48 years.

Teachings and Other Products from the Coulters

Clifton has in-depth teachings from The School of Ministry on Galatians and Romans.

Geri's set on "Victorious Christian Living" is available at a special price for *Saint or Sinner* readers: $40.00 per set (10 CDs each)

Music CD available: Clifton and Geri singing Country Gospel titled *Father's Love*

Geri's spiritual autobiography, written over a 30-year period and released in January 2016: *Your Rose Will Bloom Again* - $15.00 (Also available on Amazon in Kindle format)

Coming soon! *Nuggets from the Gold Mine* by Geri (a compilation of revelations from the Word)

Movie: *How the West Was Won* Written, directed, and produced by David Hinton. (Clifton and Geri appear as ranch owners and there is a surprise event during the story.) Sequel coming!

The Coulters may be reached by going to their
website or the church's website:
www.cliftoncoulterministries.com
www.gracefamilyoutreachchurch.com
gericoulter@aol.com
cliftoncoulter77@aol.com
Phone: 573-330-8450/8451